I0190596

Christians, Christians, Everywhere, How Do Your Gardens Grow?

A Stewardship Service
For Youth

Cynthia E. Cowen

CSS Publishing Company, Inc.
Lima, Ohio

CHRISTIANS, CHRISTIANS, EVERYWHERE, HOW DO YOUR GARDENS GROW?

Copyright © 1994 by
The CSS Publishing Company, Inc.
Lima, Ohio

All rights reserved. No part of this publication may be reproduced, stored in a retrieval system, or transmitted in any form or by any means, electronic, mechanical, photocopying, recording, or otherwise, without the prior permission of the publisher. Inquiries should be addressed to: The CSS Publishing Company, Inc., 517 South Main Street, P.O. Box 4503, Lima, Ohio 45802-4503.

0-7880-0115-9   PRINTED IN U.S.A.

This program is dedicated to the staff, volunteers, and students at Webster Elementary School, Escanaba, Michigan, whose ministry of loving, nurturing, and caring for each other in the arena of public education has taught me a lot about tilling in my own part of God's vineyard. To be a Christian, in whatever area of God's service God calls each of us to, takes a giving of ourselves in humble service and patience in planting and tilling until harvest comes. May God continue to bless their ministry in their neighborhood and community.

Goal

To enable youth to participate in a worship service based on the theme of sowing and reaping in the kingdom of God. To help participants and congregation to understand the process of growth in the giving of our talents and offerings to the work of the church.

Contents

Christians, Christians, Everywhere, How Do Your Gardens Grow?

A Service For Youth

Call To Worship:
Jesus told his disciples, "The harvest is plentiful but the workers are few. Ask the Lord of the harvest, therefore, to send out workers into his harvest field." God calls a people to come and labor in his fields to gather a harvest of souls. With thankful hearts we come to you today to give a report of our efforts here in our corner of his garden. Empower us, O Creator of the Universe, to respond to your call to help your garden grow.

Processional Hymn: "Come, You Thankful People Come"

(Children process in and sit in bunches according to crop)

Harvester: I come today as a harvester of Jesus the Christ to inspect this corner of God's garden. I ask you, as a congregation, to come along with me and inspect the condition of your garden here at *(name of church)*. God likes cheerful laborers so the children and I would like to teach you our planting song. As we journey from row to row, we'll sing this planting song repeating it twice.

Planting Song:
    Inch by inch, Row by row,
    We're going to help God's garden grow.
    We'll pull and weed and yank those stones,
    Bathe in prayer those old dry bones.

(Repeat)

Children's Chant:

Christians, Christians, everywhere, how do your gardens grow? With lots of prayer and the Word of God, we plant them row by row.

Harvester: Our first stop is the Garden of Eden. Here we behold God's creative power at work.

Reading: Genesis 2:4-9, 15-17

Harvester: What you have just heard is God's story of creation, but in this world legends have grown up surrounding the biblical story of creation. Our youth will now share one such legend from Africa with you today.

Planting Song *(Sung twice)*

(Skit players take their places)

God's Unity Garden

Planting Song *(Sung twice as group sits down)*

Harvester: God desired his creations to live in peace and harmony and had provided all that they would ever need in the Garden of Eden. This first garden overflowed with abundant provisions for their enjoyment, but the first man and woman disobeyed God's command eating the fruit of the tree which has been depicted as an apple. Let's look at the apples in your garden today.

Planting Song *(Sung twice as apples stand up)*

Song: "As We Go 'Round The Apple Tree"
(Sung to the tune of "Here We Go 'Round The Mulberry Bush")

Verse 1:
  As we go 'round the apple tree,
  The apple tree, the apple tree;
  As we go 'round the apple tree,
  We check for good ripe fruit.

Verse 2:
  In the first apple we find a worm,
  Find a worm, find a worm;
  In the first apple we find a worm,
  So we throw that fruit away.

Verse 3:
  The second apple is overripe,
  Is overripe, is overripe;
  The second apple is overripe,
  So we throw that fruit away.

Verse 4:
  The third apple is green and hard,
  Is green and hard, is green and hard;
  The third apple is green and hard,
  So we throw that fruit away.

Verse 5:
  The last apple is plump and red,
  Is plump and red, is plump and red;
  The last apple is plump and red,
  It's been nourished and well fed.

Verse 6:
  The whole world will look up to us,
  Look up to us, look up to us;
  The whole world will look up to us,
  As our faith matures and grows.

Harvester: Checking out this crop of apples, I find that there is a worm in the first. The cares and worries of the world seem to have crept into it and eaten it away. The second is overripe which happens when we take our faith for granted and become complacent and mushy inside. The third apple is green and hard. It has refused to ripen and has ignored God's call to come to church, to attend Sunday school, to pray, and to give. It's core has become hardened to the Spirit. But the last apple is plump and red. It has been fed in prayer and study in order to be ready for the Harvester to pick. Let's pray that the remaining crop matures and grows in their knowledge of Jesus Christ as Lord.

Planting Song *(Sung twice as apples sit down)*

Children's Chant:
Christians, Christians, everywhere, how do your gardens grow? With lots of prayer and the Word of God, we plant them row by row.

Reading: Matthew 21:18-21

Harvester: We must be continually alert to Christ's coming to inspect the fruit of our lives. He plants us through baptism into his garden. In the church we are fed and watered as we participate in all areas of congregational life. But we do have to respond to God's call to grow. Let's look at our fig tree and see how it's growing.

Planting Song *(Sung twice as figs stand up)*

Song: "O, Bare Fig Tree"
(Sung to the tune of "O, Christmas Tree")

(Children wave bare branches for verse 1)

Verse 1:
    O, bare fig tree, O, bare fig tree,
    How ugly are your branches.
    O, bare fig tree, O, bare fig tree,
    How ugly are your branches.

You did not yield when Christ passed by,
And consequently, chose to die.
O, bare fig tree, O, bare fig tree,
How ugly are your branches.

Verse 2:
O, Jesus Christ, O, Jesus Christ,
We pray for your anointing.
O, Jesus Christ, O, Jesus Christ,
We pray for your empowering.
We want to bear for you the best.
We need your help to do the rest.
O, Jesus Christ, O, Jesus Christ,
We bring forth fruit a'plenty.
(Children bring out branches loaded with figs)

Planting Song *(Sung twice as fig trees sit down)*

Children's Chant:
Christians, Christians, everywhere, how do your gardens grow? With lots of prayer and the Word of God, we plant them row by row.

Reading: Matthew 13:24-29

Harvester: In our corner of the garden there will be weeds which the enemy will sow to bring about discord. They seek to choke the Word of Christ out of our spirits. Jesus tells us that they are to grow alongside our wheat so that the wheat is not yanked out if we try to rid ourselves of the weed. Let's look at your garden and see if this is happening.

Planting Song *(Sung twice as weeds and buds sit up)*

Song: "I'm An Ugly Weed"
(Sung to the tune of "I'm An Old Cowhand")

Verse 1:
    I'm an ugly weed from a world of cares,
    I will prick your soul and cause grey hairs!
    I will plant hate and fear if you give me room;
    I will spread doubt and grief
    Which will cause great gloom;
    I will fight to destroy all those Christian blooms;
    Give me a world of care; give me a world of care.

Verse 2:
    We are Christian buds that delight to bloom.
    We don't need you weeds and won't give you room.
    We will strive with our souls to reach out in love.
    We will meet the onslaught with an iron glove.
    We will speak forth God's Word in power and love.
    Lord, help us to love and care;
    Help us to love and care.

Planting Song *(Sung twice as weeds and buds sit down)*

Children's Chant:
    Christians, Christians, everywhere, how do your gardens grow? With lots of prayer and the Word of God, we plant them row by row.

Reading: Matthew 13:3b-9

Harvester: Jesus taught the importance of the soil in his garden. The seed sown along the path is received by the hearts which hear God's message but don't understand it. Satan comes and snatches the good news away. The seed sown on rocky places is received by the heart who hears the Word and rejoices at it, but being a heart which is shallow and lacks deep roots, the message lasts only a short time. Troubles and persecutions cause this person to quickly fall away from faith. The heart that received the seed which fell among thorns is the one who hears the Word but allows the worries of this life and the deceitfulness of wealth to choke it out, making it unfruitful. But the heart which receives the seed that fell on good soil is the one which hears the Word and understands it. The crop produced from good soil planting will yield 100, 60 or 30 times what was sown. So the condition of the soil in your garden is very important. Let's check out the workers as they till your soil.

Planting Song *(Sung twice as workers with hoes stand)*

Song: "Till, Till, Till The Soil"
(Sung to the tune of "Row, Row, Row Your Boat")

Verse 1:
>   Till, till, till the soil,
>   'til it's fertile ground.
>   Eagerly, eagerly, eagerly, eagerly,
>   Let your love abound.

Verse 2:
>   Plant, plant, plant the seed,
>   In the hearts of all.
>   Merrily, merrily, merrily, merrily,
>   Christ is all in all.

Verse 3:
>   Pull, pull, pull those weeds,
>   'til they disappear.
>   Joyfully, joyfully, joyfully, joyfully,
>   See the sprouts appear.

Verse 4:
>   Soak, soak, soak the ground;
>   Bathe it now in prayer.
>   Happily, happily, happily, happily,
>   We give it special care.

Verse 5:
>   Reap, reap, reap the crop,
>   Watch as Satan flops.
>   Thankfully, thankfully, thankfully, thankfully,
>   Jesus Christ is tops!

Planting Song *(Sung twice as workers sit down)*

Children's Chant:
Christians, Christians, everywhere, how do your gardens grow? With lots of prayer and the Word of God, we plant them row by row.

Harvester: As workers till the ground so God blesses their labor. We in God's church work together to reach out to all people. We now take this time to return to God a portion of our earthly blessings, the fruit of our labors.

Offering *(Children pass bushel baskets while people sing)*

Offering Hymn: "Praise And Thanksgiving"

Harvester: We present to you, O gracious God, our tithes and offerings. Multiply it for your use in the kingdom.

All: Amen.

Offertory: "Praise God From Whom All Blessings Flow"

Harvester: Let us continue our journey and inspect another section of your garden. Look at that field of wheat!

Children's Chant:
Christians, Christians, everywhere, how do your gardens grow? With lots of prayer and the Word of God, we plant them row by row.

Reading: John 12:23-25

Planting Song *(Sung twice as wheat rises)*

Song: "Little Joseph Had A Dream"
(Sung to the tune of "There Was A Farmer Had A Dog, And Bingo Was His Name-O")

Verse 1:
    Little Joseph had a dream
    And dreamt of wheat bent down-O.
    W - H - E - A - T, W - H - E - A - T,
    W - H - E - A - T, and dreamt of wheat bent down-O.

(Wave wheat and then bend it down)

Verse 2:
    Older Joseph saw that dream
    Come true in God's own time-O.
    D - R - E - A - M, D - R - E - A - M,
    D - R - E - A - M, come true in God's own time-O.

Verse 3:
    Young and old unite in Christ
    And bow before your Maker.
    M - A - K - E - R, M - A - K - E - R,
    M - A - K - E - R, bow down before your Maker.
(Children bow down)

Planting Song *(Sung twice as wheat sits down)*

Harvester: Little Joseph wore a coat of many colors. He was the favorite son of his father, Jacob. God spoke to him in dreams, but he boasted too much. His brothers turned on him in their jealousy and sold him into slavery. But God had a plan! In his time, he raised Joseph to a position of power second only to Pharaoh in Egypt. God has no favorites in Christ. Young and old, we work to produce a harvest for God. But it will come in his time. The important thing is for us to work in harmony with others in the field. How can we do that? Let's hear from another product of the field, our heads of lettuce who will share how we should work.

15

Children's Chant:

Christians, Christians, everywhere, how do your gardens grow? With lots of prayer and the Word of God, we plant them row by row.

Reading: Romans 12:3-16

Planting Song *(Sung twice as the lettuce rises)*

Song: "Lettuce Break Ground Together On Our Knees" *(Sung to the tune of "Let Us Break Bread Together On Our Knees")*

Verse 1:
> Lettuce break ground together on our knees.
> Lettuce break ground together on our knees.
> When I fall down on my knees, with my face to the Son above, O, Christ, have mercy on me.

Verse 2:
> Lettuce plant gifts of caring all around.
> Lettuce plant gifts of caring all around.
> When I fall down on my knees, with my face to the Son above, O, Christ, have mercy on me.

Verse 3:
> Lettuce praise God together on our knees.
> Lettuce praise God together on our knees.
> When I come to the throne on high, with
>   my bushel basket piled high,
> The Lord will be happy with me.

Planting Song *(Sung twice as lettuce sits)*

Harvester: We near the end of our garden. Let us now hear from one of our young harvesters who recently heard some of our produce talking.

Children's Chant:
Christians, Christians, everywhere, how do your gardens grow? With lots of prayer and the Word of God, we plant it row by row.

Reading: Galatians 5:22-23

Planting Song *(Sung once as young harvester rises)*

Stop Vegetating *(Meditation delivered by a young harvester)*

Planting Song *(Sung once as young harvester sits down)*

Harvester: We need to remember to stop vegetating and be about producing the right produce for God, but what about our own spiritual gardens? We cannot ignore the fruits that the Holy Spirit will produce in our lives if we allow him to plant the life of Christ within us. Look at these children. What do you see? LOVE *(poster held up in one section)*, JOY *(poster held up in another)*, PEACE *(poster)*, PATIENCE *(poster)*, KINDNESS *(poster)*, GOODNESS *(poster)*, FAITHFULNESS *(poster)*, GENTLENESS *(poster)*, and SELF-CONTROL *(poster)*. Truly you have a garden to applaud.

All: Clap

Harvester: Jesus said, "I am the true vine, and my Father is the gardener." Then he tells us that he is the vine and we are the branches and if we remain connected to him, and he lives within our hearts, we will bear much fruit, fruit that will endure. Apart from Jesus we can do nothing. Go forth today and plant your gardens in love. Till the soil, water with your sweat and tears, fertilize in prayer, study and giving, and reap a beautiful bumper crop for Jesus.

Recessional Hymn: "For The Beauty Of The Earth"

Songs

PLANTING SONG:

Inch by inch, Row by row,
We're going to help God's garden grow.
We'll pull and weed and yank those stones,
Bathe in prayer those old dry bones.
(Repeat)

Tune:

"As We Go 'Round The Apple Tree"
(Sung to the tune of "Here We Go 'Round The Mulberry Bush")

Verse 1:
    As we go 'round the apple tree,
    The apple tree, the apple tree;
    As we go 'round the apple tree,
    We check for good ripe fruit.

Verse 2:
    In the first apple we find a worm,
    Find a worm, find a worm;
    In the first apple we find a worm,
    So we throw that fruit away.

Verse 3:
    The second apple is overripe,
    Is overripe, is overripe;
    The second apple is overripe,
    So we throw that fruit away.

Verse 4:
    The third apple is green and hard,
    Is green and hard, is green and hard;
    The third apple is green and hard,
    So we throw that fruit away.

Verse 5:
    The last apple is plump and red,
    Is plump and red, is plump and red;
    The last apple is plump and red,
    It's been nourished and well fed.

Verse 6:
    The whole world will look up to us,
    Look up to us, look up to us;
    The whole world will look up to us,
    As our faith matures and grows.

"O, Bare Fig Tree"
(Sung to the tune of "O, Christmas Tree")

Verse 1:
    O, bare fig tree, O, bare fig tree,
    How ugly are your branches.
    O, bare fig tree, O, bare fig tree,
    How ugly are your branches.
    You did not yield when Christ passed by,
    And consequently, chose to die.
    O, bare fig tree, O bare fig tree,
    How ugly are your branches.

Verse 2:
    O, Jesus Christ, O, Jesus Christ,
    We pray for your anointing.
    O, Jesus Christ, O, Jesus Christ,
    We pray for your empowering.
    We want to bear for you the best.
    We need your help to do the rest.
    O, Jesus Christ, O, Jesus Christ,
    We bring forth fruit a'plenty.

"I'm An Ugly Weed"
(Sung to the tune of "I'm An Old Cowhand")

Verse 1:
    I'm an ugly weed from a world of cares,
    I will prick your soul and cause grey hairs!
    I will plant hate and fear if you give me room;
    I will spread doubt and grief
    Which will cause great gloom;
    I will fight to destroy all those Christian blooms;
    Give me a world of care; give me a world of care.

Verse 2:
 We are Christian buds that delight to bloom.
 We don't need you weeds and won't give you room.
 We will strive with our souls to reach out in love.
 We will meet the onslaught with an iron glove.
 We will speak forth God's Word in power and love.
 Lord, help us to love and care;
 Help us to love and care.

"Till, Till, Till The Soil"
(Sung to the tune of "Row, Row, Row Your Boat")
Verse 1:
 Till, till, till the soil,
 'til it's fertile ground.
 Eagerly, eagerly, eagerly, eagerly,
 Let your love abound.
Verse 2:
 Plant, plant, plant the seed,
 In the hearts of all.
 Merrily, merrily, merrily, merrily,
 Christ is all in all.
Verse 3:
 Pull, pull, pull those weeds,
 'til they disappear.
 Joyfully, joyfully, joyfully, joyfully,
 See the sprouts appear.
Verse 4:
 Soak, soak, soak the ground;
 Bathe it now in prayer.
 Happily, happily, happily, happily,
 We give it special care.
Verse 5:
 Reap, reap, reap the crop,
 Watch as Satan flops.
 Thankfully, thankfully, thankfully, thankfully,
 Jesus Christ is tops!

"Little Joseph Had A Dream"
(Sung to the tune of "There Was A Farmer Had A Dog, And Bingo Was His Name-O")

Verse 1:

Little Joseph had a dream
And dreamt of wheat bent down-O.
W - H - E - A - T, W - H - E - A - T,
W - H - E - A - T, and dreamt of wheat bent down-O.

(Wave wheat and then bend it down)

Verse 2:

Older Joseph saw that dream
Come true in God's own time-O.
D - R - E - A - M, D - R - E - A - M,
D - R - E - A - M, come true in God's own time-O.

Verse 3:

Young and old unite in Christ
And bow before your Maker.
M - A - K - E - R, M - A - K - E - R,
M - A - K - E - R, bow down before your Maker.

"Lettuce Break Ground Together On Our Knees"
(Sung to the tune of "Let Us Break Bread Together On Our Knees")

Verse 1:

Lettuce break ground together on our knees.
Lettuce break ground together on our knees.
When I fall down on my knees, with my face to the
Son above, O, Christ, have mercy on me.

Verse 2:

Lettuce plant gifts of caring all around.
Lettuce plant gifts of caring all around.
When I fall down on my knees, with my face to the
Son above, O, Christ, have mercy on me.

Verse 3:

Lettuce praise God together on our knees.
Lettuce praise God together on our knees.
When I come to the throne on high, with
my bushel basket piled high,
The Lord will be happy with me.

Suggested Hymns:

"Come, You Thankful People Come"
"Praise And Thanksgiving"
"Praise God From Whom All Blessings Flow"
"For The Beauty Of The Earth"

Props And Costumes

God's Unity Garden
Assorted body parts: ears, eyes, hands, feet, mouths, tongues, noses, legs, arms, stomach, fingers, necks, knees, chins, toes, backbone, teeth (posters depicting each item can be created). Creator God can use a hoe.

Apple Group
May use a big bushel basket and pull out an apple with a worm, an overripe apple, a green apple, and a plump, red apple. Children can dress in red and have apple costumes. May construct a tree for children to march around.

Fig Group
Children can dress in brown with white socks on hands and feet to look like trees and carry bare branches which they wave for first verse. Second verse have branches with figs loaded. Costumes can also be constructed to look like figs.

Weeds And Blooms Group
May divide the group up into ugly weeds (wear grey and make thistles, dandelions, weeds of different kinds). Buds can be flowers and blooms of sorts. Two different worlds can be used as a prop and held up by a child: One globe with a black cloud and word, CARE. One globe with a heart attached and the word, CARE.

Tillers Group
Children can dress as farmers and use hoes, rakes, shovels, and watering cans. Bushel baskets can be used for reaping.

Wheat Group
Sheets spelling out W-H-E-A-T, D-R-E-A-M, and M-A-K-E-R can be made and held up as each letter is sung. Children can dress in black and white. Another option is to have little robes of many colors.

Lettuce Group

Children can dress in green and have costumes of lettuce leaves or heads of lettuce attached.

Fruits Of The Spirit

Posters can be made using different fruits and having spiritual fruit written on it: love (tomato), joy (lemon), peace (peas), patience (grapes), kindness (orange), goodness (apple), faithfulness (banana), gentleness (pear), and self-control (pineapple).

Optional Banner Or Flannelgraph Display

Design a banner or flannelgraph board to go along with the theme. Possible suggestions:

Be Ripe For Jesus
Be Ready For Jesus
Be Weeded For Jesus
Bud For Jesus
Dig For Jesus
Harvest For Jesus
Die To Jesus!

"Let us come to Jesus and be fruitful!"

How Does Your Garden Grow?

Be Ripe for Jesus
 Be Ready for Jesus
Be Weeded for Jesus
 Bud for Jesus
Dig for Jesus
Harvest for
    Jesus
Die to Jesus!

"Let us come to Jesus
✝ Be fruitful!

God's Unity Garden

There is an old African legend which tells the story of creation. It seems like the Creator God decided to plant a garden upon his newly-formed planet Earth. He picked out a suitable plot, tilled the soil, and planted rows and rows of a variety of body parts. There was a row of ears, of eyes, of hands, of feet, of mouths, of tongues, of noses, of legs, of arms, and right in the middle of the garden he planted a stomach. Now after he had finished his planting, he stepped back to watch his garden grow. When all the parts had successfully broken through the fertile soil and had begun to flourish, he walked through his garden again eyeing his creations with admiration. When he felt they could survive without his tender cultivating, he asked them if they would grow together now in peace and harmony.

"No problem," said the mouths who were the spokespersons for the group. "We'll handle this situation fine," replied the hands waving the Creator God a fond farewell. The heads nodded their approval while the fingers gave the A-okay sign.

The Creator God looked back and nodded, giving his blessing to the garden, and left to be about creating other parts of the universe. No sooner had he disappeared over the edge of the earth than his creations in the garden started to get into trouble with each other.

The noses started poking around in the other body parts' personal business. The eyes started wandering and coveting things which they should not have desired which caused the hands to start grabbing for things which did not belong to them. The ears started to eavesdrop on the others' conversations which caused the tongues to wag even more as the lips flapped away. The arms overextended their reach and caused the upper body parts to give cold shoulders to their neighbors. The necks stretched to see what was happening in their neighbors' backyards causing the chins to be lifted in self-righteous pride over their favored positions. The feet started tromping on the toes. The legs began to ache in discontent while the knees knocked at the furor which was arising from the group. The arms began to wave about putting the necks out of joint.

The Creator God had just reached the edge of the universe when he heard this great commotion. He quickly sped back to his garden to find out what the cause was. When he arrived he was astonished to find quarreling and grumbling. "What happened to you, my children? You promised to live in peace and harmony with yourselves."

The body parts all hung limp in shame blaming each other, especially the feet, for overstepping their bounds. The fingers started pointing at others in accusation. The stomach just sat there and said, "I didn't do anything but sit here" — which was true. He hadn't even rumbled while the others went on with their excuses. But then the Creator God boomed out, "I can see that you need my assistance in coming together so I will make sure that you have to cooperate with each other." He bent down and went down the rows gathering parts from all over the garden and attaching them to each other. The hands, feet, eyes, ears, legs, and arms wanted to stay in pairs since they had grown as twins. So the Creator God agreed that he would not separate them. He put the toes on the feet and connected them to the legs placing the knees in the middle to stop them from knocking in fear. He gave the backbone a surge of strength and connected the fingers to the hands to the arms to the shoulders allowing the neck to join the head and planted the ears, eyes, nose, and mouth on the face. He had the mouth open wide to install the tongue and the chattering teeth. He placed the stomach in the middle since he had not been a disruptive force.

Looking at his new creation, the Creator God stepped back and said, "Now you need a group project to build your unity. Hmmm . . . I know: feed the stomach!" "Feed the stomach?" the body questioned. "Yes, feed the stomach," the Creator God commanded. "Sounds good to me," the stomach rumbled. And that is what has been occurring ever since.

The eyes search for new foods, the nose sniffs out the aromas, the mouth opens to take in the various shapes, the tongue distinguishes the flavors, the ears are aware of the sounds of food, the neck helps to turn in the direction the feet and legs take to help the hands and arms recover the items that the fingers can pick up. Even the knees bend so that the body can pull the items from the earth. All the parts work in harmony to gather food to feed the stomach who remains in the middle relishing each item that enters it.

Peace and harmony had come to the Garden of the Creator God. He was so pleased that he decided to create more of these bodies. So now we come in a variety of shapes, sizes, and colors with a definite purpose and we are still seeking to live in peace and harmony in the Creator God's garden.

Meditation

Stop Your Vegetating

Read Romans 12:3-16

> *Just as each of us has one body with many members, and*
> *these members do not all have the same function, so in*
> *Christ we who are many form one body, and each mem-*
> *ber belongs to all the others.* — Romans 12:4-5

The plight of the farmer had drawn all the vegetables together in the root cellar of his home for the first time in the annals of their history. "I've called you all here tonight," announced the acorn squash, "to squash these rumors that there is a strain on our community." "But there is," the onion pealed out. "I could just cry when I think of the economic plight of our farmer. Tears brim up from under my thin skin." "I'm boiling mad and could mash all of you," the potato sputtered. "Look at my red eyes. I'm tired of trying to sprout a solution all on my own." "Well, I thought I could certainly turn up an answer to this pickle he's in," replied the turnip. "Beats me what all this fussing's about. My greens added color to his dull meal tonight," the beet pridefully blushed red. "Shucks, I've been all ears, listening to each of you trying to solve our caregiver's dilemma tonight," drawled the ear of corn. "Let me give you some kernels of advice." The corn's silky hair and erect stalk gave him a certain amount of credibility among the rows of vegetables assembled. "We have all been doing our own thing, not taking into consideration the hard labor and love that the farmer gives us. He carefully plants, cultivates, waters, weeds out that which might harm us, and then harvests us when we are ripe for picking. We need to cooperate in the only way we know how now to make his life a little more profitable. We can combine our efforts to give him a bumper crop this season. We can come together to arrange a delicious meal for him to feast on. We can stop

31

vegetating and start producing for the one who tenderly cares for us. For all he has done for us, certainly uniting together is not a difficult response.'' They all agreed that night to take the corn's advice, and though the farmer did not become wealthy that first year, through continued effort, in time his harvest became more plentiful.

Christ calls us to set aside our differences and unite to further his kingdom here on earth. God has carefully planted the life of Jesus in us, cultivated it with his Word, watered it in his love, and weeded out sin which would choke out our very existence. Our response as we work in unity will yield souls won to a saving knowledge of Jesus Christ. He stated that unless a kernel of wheat falls to the ground and dies, it remains only a seed. He died that we might have abundant life. We need to die to ourselves so we can become part of those who labor at planting, those who till the soil, and those who are blessed to harvest his crops. Stop vegetating and start cultivating your corner of the garden so as to yield a bumper crop for Jesus this year!

Bulletin For Service

Christians, Christians, Everywhere, How Do Your Gardens Grow?

A Service For Youth

Call To Worship:
Jesus told his disciples, "The harvest is plentiful but the workers are few. Ask the Lord of the harvest, therefore, to send out workers into his harvest field." God calls a people to come and labor in his fields to gather a harvest of souls. With thankful hearts we come to you today to give a report of our efforts here in our corner of his garden. Empower us, O Creator of the Universe, to respond to your call to help your garden grow.

Hymn: "Come, You Thankful People Come"

Harvester Speaks
Planting Song:
Inch by inch, Row by row,
We're going to help God's garden grow.
We'll pull and weed and yank those stones,
Bathe in prayer those old dry bones.
(Repeat)

Children's Chant
Harvester Speaks

God's Garden

Reading: Genesis 2:4-9, 15-17

Harvester Speaks
Planting Song *(Sung twice)*

God's Unity Garden

Planting Song *(Sung twice as group sits down)*

33

What's In Your Garden?

Harvester Speaks
Planting Song *(Sung twice as apples rise)*

Song: "As We Go 'Round The Apple Tree"

Harvester Speaks
Planting Song *(Sung twice as apples sit down)*
Children's Chant

Reading: Matthew 21:18-21

Harvester Speaks
Planting Song *(Sung twice as figs rise)*

Song: "O, Bare Fig Tree"

Planting Song *(Sung twice as figs sit down)*
Children's Chant

Reading: Matthew 13:24-29

Harvester Speaks
Planting Song *(Sung twice for weeds and buds)*

Song: "I'm An Ugly Weed"

Planting Song *(Sung twice as weeds and buds sit down)*
Children's Chant

Reading: Matthew 13:3b-9

Harvester Speaks

Planting Song *(Sung twice as workers rise)*

Song: "Till, Till, Till The Soil"

Planting Song *(Sung twice as workers sit down)*
Children's Chant
Harvester Speaks

A Tithe From Our Gardens

Offering Received

Offering Hymn: "Praise And Thanksgiving"

Harvester Speaks:
    We present to you, O gracious God, our tithes and offerings. Multiply it for your use in the kingdom.
All: Amen.

Offertory: "Praise God From Whom All Blessings Flow"

A Good Crop

Harvester Speaks
Children's Chant

Reading: John 12:23-25

Planting Song *(Sung twice as wheat rises)*

Song: "Little Joseph Had A Dream"

Planting Song *(Sung twice as wheat sits)*
Harvester Speaks
Children's Chant

Reading: Romans 12:3-16

Planting Song *(Sung twice as lettuce rises)*

Song: "Lettuce Break Ground Together"

Planting Song *(Sung twice as lettuce sits)*
Harvester Speaks
Children's Chant

35

Reading: Galatians 5:22-23

Planting Song *(Sung once for young harvester)*

Meditation: Stop Vegetating

Planting Song *(Sung once as harvester sits)*
Harvester Speaks

Hymn: "For The Beauty Of The Earth"

www.ingramcontent.com/pod-product-compliance
Lightning Source LLC
Chambersburg PA
CBHW071801020426
42331CB00008B/2350